UKULELE

CHART HITS OF 2019 2020

ISBN 978-1-5400-8507-8

Visit Hal Leonard Online at
www.halleonard.com

Contact us:
Hal Leonard
7777 West Bluemound Road
Milwaukee, WI 53213
Email: info@halleonard.com

In Europe, contact:
Hal Leonard Europe Limited
42 Wigmore Street
Marylebone, London, W1U 2RN
Email: info@halleonardeurope.com

In Australia, contact:
Hal Leonard Australia Pty. Ltd.
4 Lentara Court
Cheltenham, Victoria, 3192 Australia
Email: info@halleonard.com.au

Beautiful People

Words and Music by Ed Sheeran, Khalid Robinson, Fred Gibson, Max Martin and Shellback

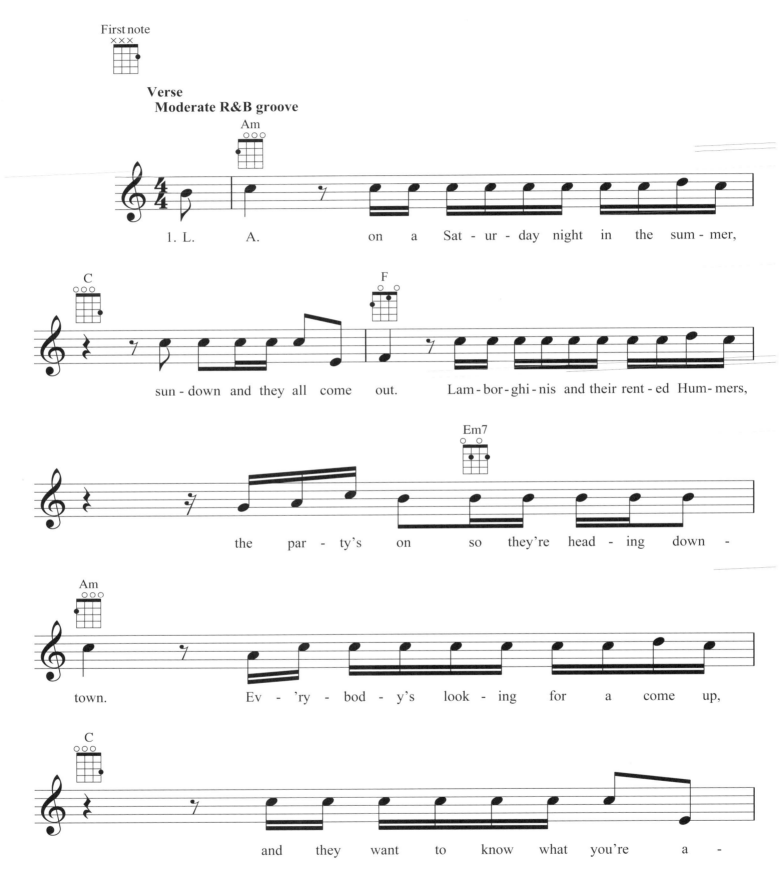

bout.　Me　in　the　mid - dle　with　the　one　I　love　and

Pre-Chorus

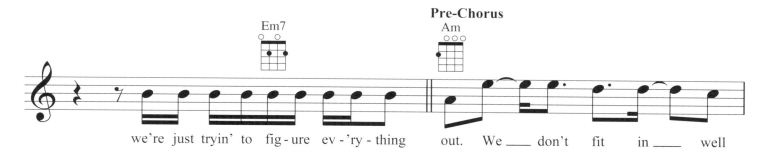

we're　just　tryin'　to　fig - ure　ev - 'ry - thing　out.　We ___ don't　fit　in ___ well

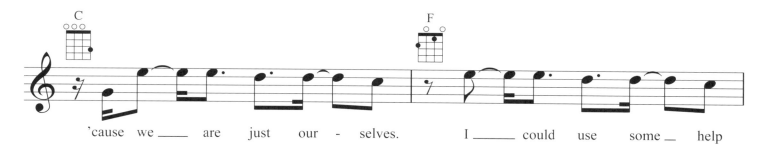

'cause　we ___ are　just　our - selves.　I ___ could　use　some __ help

get - ting　out　of　this　con - ver - sa - tion,　yeah.　You __ look　stun - ning, __ dear,

so　don't　ask　that　ques - tion ___ here.　This　is　my　on - ly ___ fear:

N.C.

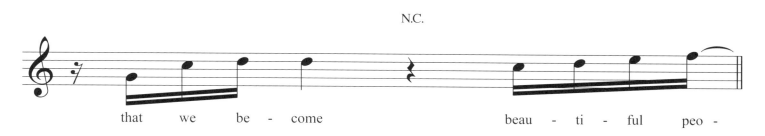

that　we　be - come　beau - ti - ful　peo -

Chorus

- ple. Drop — top, de - sign - er clothes, front — row at fash - ion shows.

"What d'you — do and who d'you know?" In - side the world of beau - ti - ful peo -

- ple. Cham - pagne and rolled - up notes, pre - nups and bro - ken homes.

Sur - round - ed but still a - lone, let's — leave the par - ty. That's not

who we are. ___ (We are, ___ we are, ___ we are.) ___ We are ___ not

beau - ti - ful. ___ Yeah, that's — not who we are. ___ (We are, ___

we ___ are just our - selves. I ___ could use some ___ help

get - ting out of this con - ver - sa - tion, yeah. You ___ look stun - ning, ___ dear,

so don't ask that ques - tion ___ here. This is my on - ly ___ fear: ___

___ that we be - come beau - ti - ful peo -

(We are, ___ we are, ___ we are.) ___ We are ___ not

beau - ti - ful. ___

Good as Hell

Words and Music by Lizzo and Eric Frederic

First note

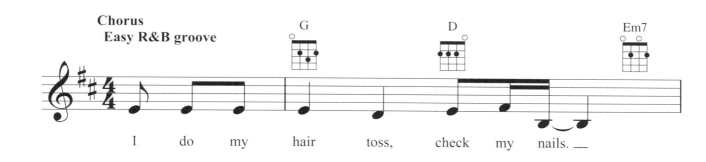

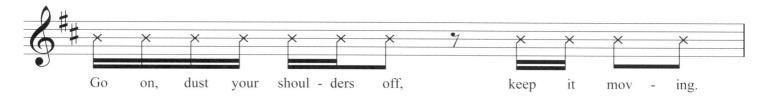

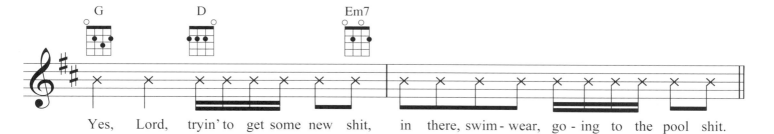

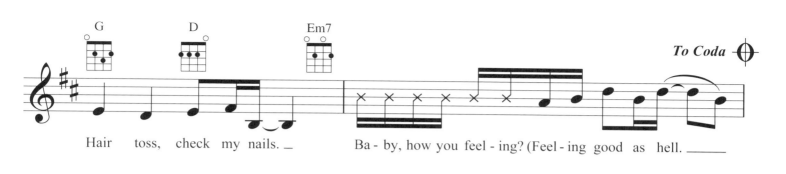

To Coda ⊕

Hair toss, check my nails. _ Ba - by, how you feel - ing? (Feel - ing good as hell. _____

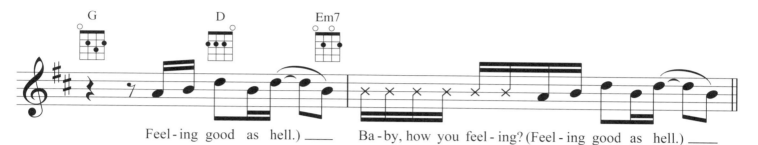

Feel - ing good as hell.) _____ Ba - by, how you feel - ing? (Feel - ing good as hell.) _____

Verse

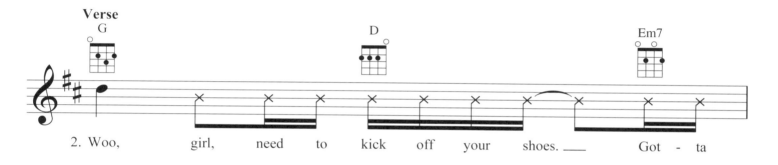

2. Woo, girl, need to kick off your shoes. ___ Got - ta

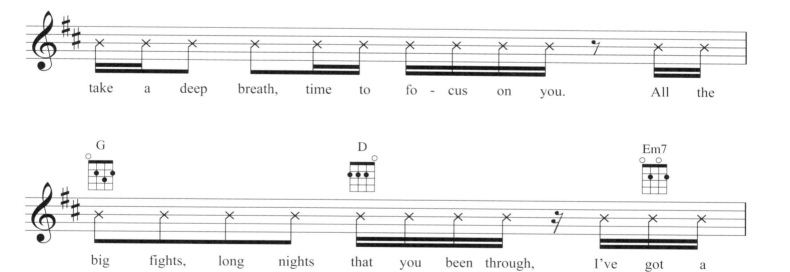

take a deep breath, time to fo - cus on you. All the

big fights, long nights that you been through, I've got a

D.S. al Coda

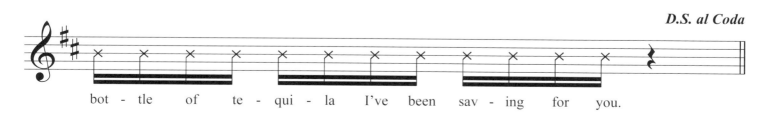

bot - tle of te - qui - la I've been sav - ing for you.

11

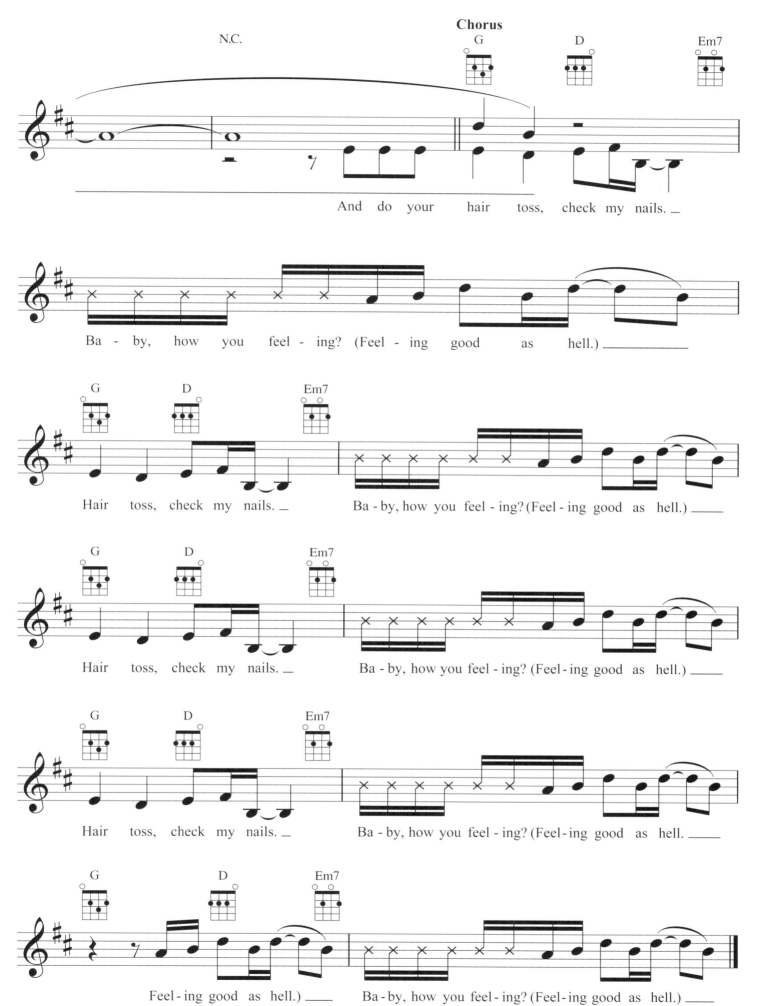

Blinding Lights

Words and Music by Abel Tesfaye, Max Martin, Jason Quenneville, Oscar Holter and Ahmad Balshe

Circles

Words and Music by Austin Post, Kaan Gunesberk, Louis Bell, William Walsh and Adam Feeney

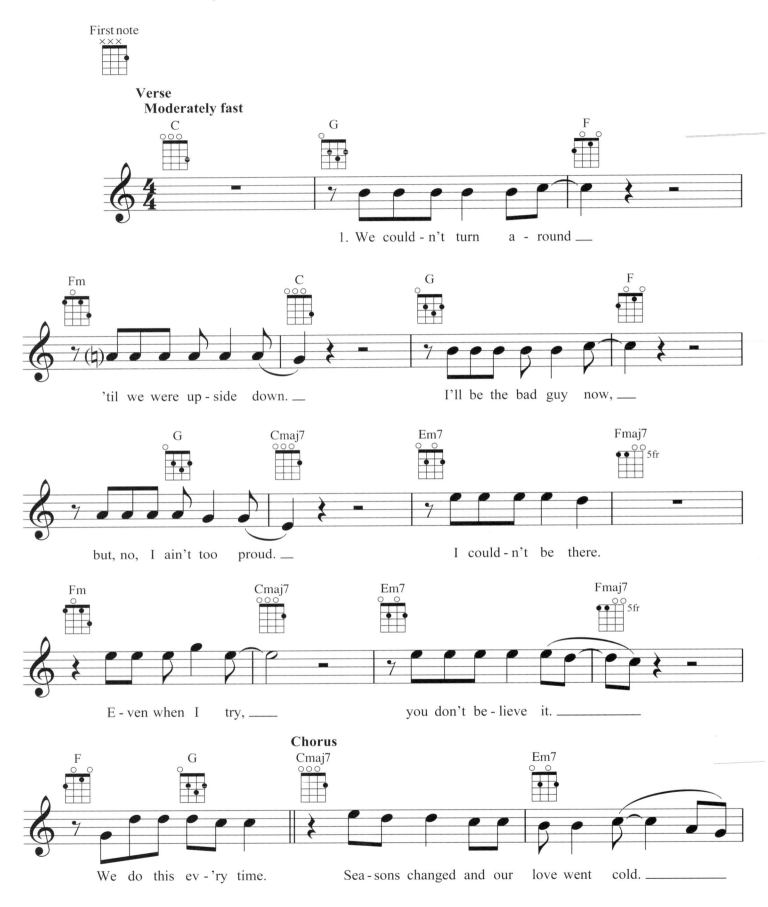

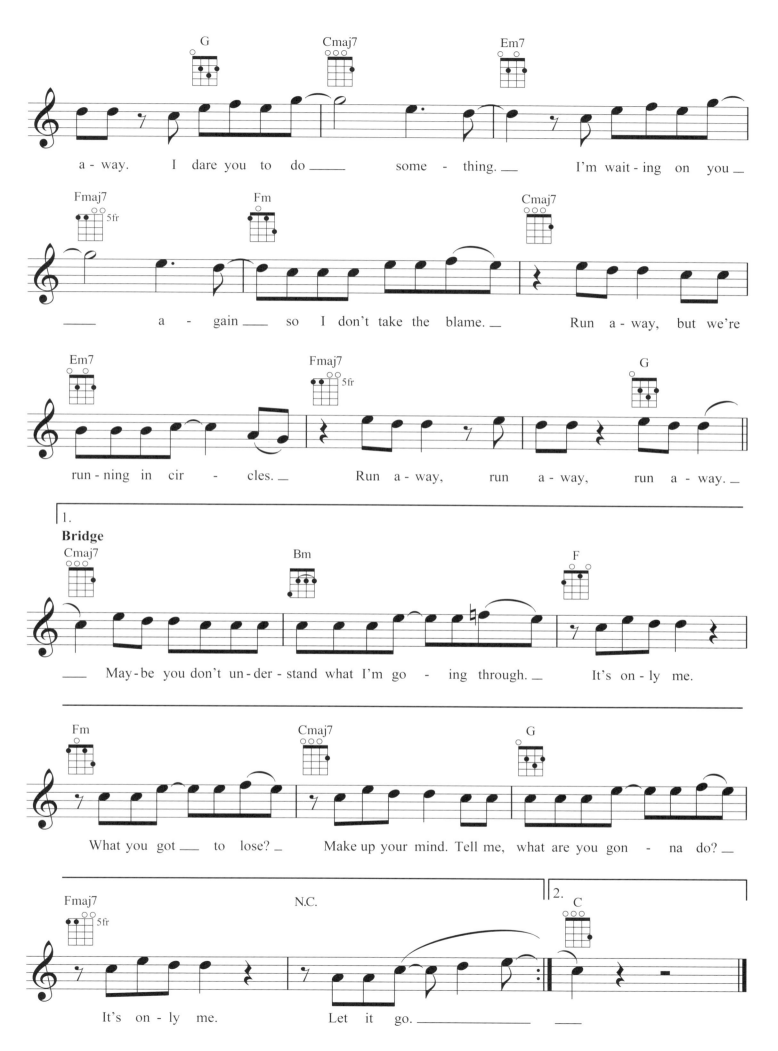

Dance Monkey

Words and Music by Toni Watson

_I, I, ___ I like ___ your style. You, you_

_make me, make me, make me want to cry, ___ and now I beg ____

_to see ___ you dance ___ just one ___ more time. So they say:_

𝄋 Chorus

_Dance for me, dance for me, dance for me, oh, oh. ___ I've nev - er seen ____

_an - y - bod - y do the ___ things you do be - fore. ___ They say:_

Move for me, move for me, move for me, ay, ay. ____ And when you're done, ____

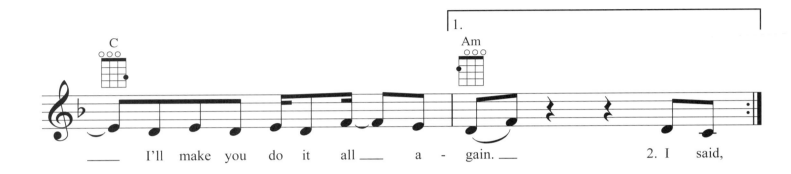

1.

____ I'll make you do it all ____ a - gain. ____ 2. I said,

2., 3. **Chorus**

gain. ____ They say: Dance for me, dance for me, dance for me, oh, oh. ____

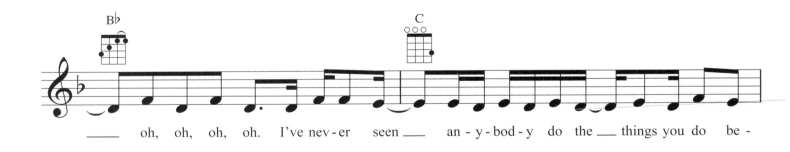

____ oh, oh, oh, oh. I've nev - er seen ____ an - y - bod - y do the ____ things you do be -

fore. ____ They say: Move for me, move for me, move for me, ay, ay. ____

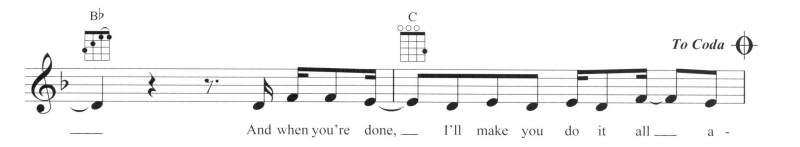

And when you're done, ___ I'll make you do it all ___ a-

Bridge

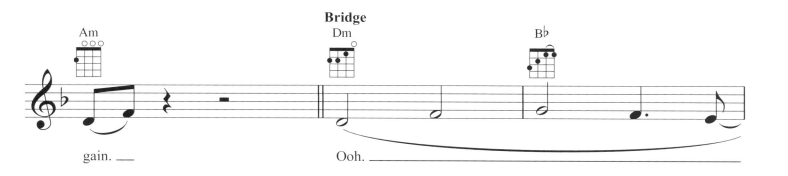

gain. ___   Ooh. ___

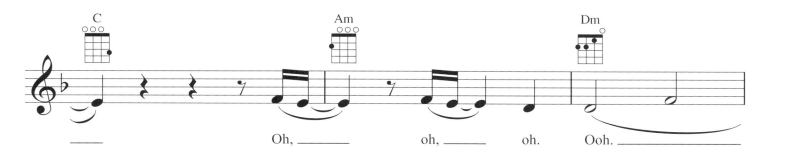

___ Oh, ___ oh, ___ oh. Ooh. ___

___   Ooh, oh, oh. They say:

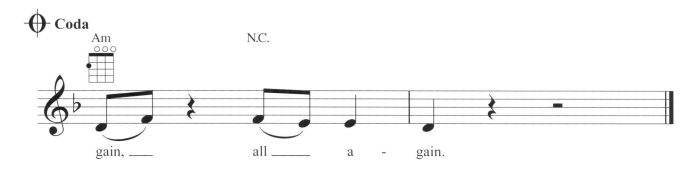

gain, ___   all ___ a - gain.

Don't Start Now

Words and Music by Dua Lipa, Caroline Ailin, Ian Kirkpatrick and Emily Schwartz

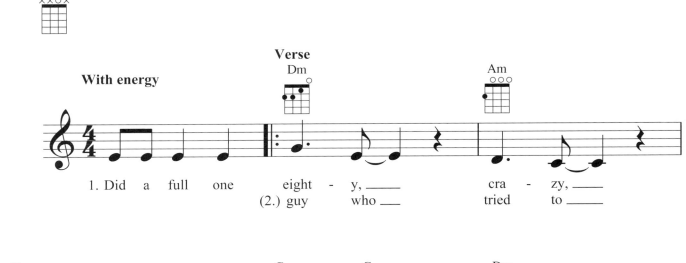

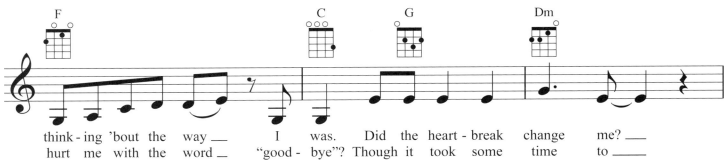

think-ing 'bout the way ___ I was. Did the heart - break change me? ___
hurt me with the word ___ "good - bye"? Though it took some time to ___

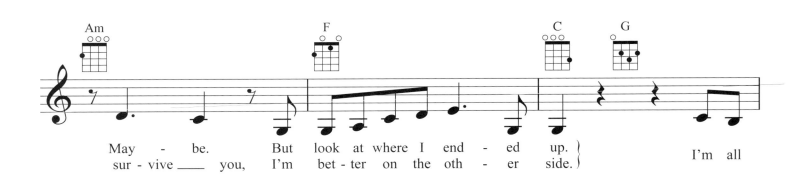

May - be. But look at where I end - ed up.
sur - vive ___ you, I'm bet - ter on the oth - er side.   I'm all

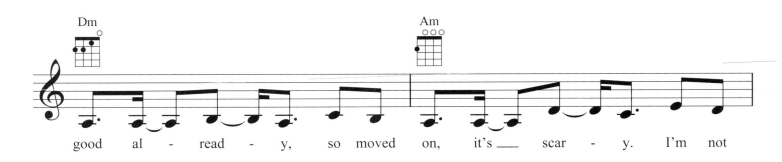

good al - read - y, so moved on, it's ___ scar - y. I'm not

way;   you ___ know   how.   Don't ___ start

1.

car - ing ___ a - bout ___ me   now.   2. Aren't   you   the

2.   **Interlude**

now.   (Up, ___ up, ___ don't come out.

Don't   show   up,   up, ___ up. ___   Don't ___ start   now,   oh.

Up, ___ up, ___   don't   come   out.)   I'm   not

D.S. al Coda

where   you ___ left ___ me   at   all. ___   So, ___

Everything I Wanted

Words and Music by Billie Eilish O'Connell and Finneas O'Connell

Goodbyes

**Words and Music by Austin Post, Brian Lee, Louis Bell, William Walsh,
Jeffrey Lamar Williams, Val Blavatnik and Jessie Lauren Foutz**

First note

Verse
Moderately slow

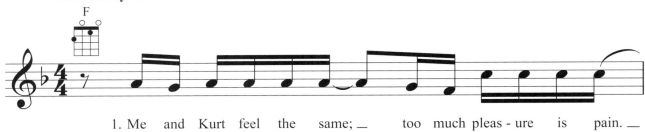

1. Me and Kurt feel the same; __ too much plea - sure is pain. __

__ My girl spites me in vain, __ all I do is com - plain, __

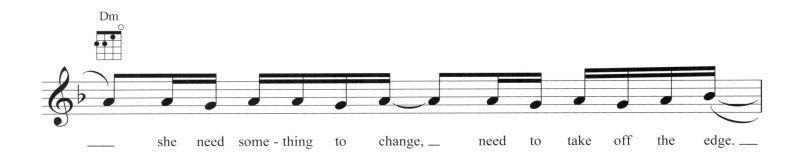

__ she need some - thing to change, __ need to take off the edge. __

_____ So fuck it all _____ to - night.

Pre-Chorus

Chorus

Your Bar - bie life doll, _____ it's Nick - i Mi - naj. _____

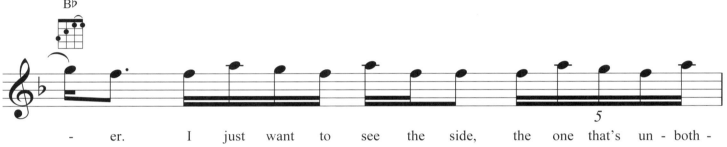

_____ You don't need a key to drive; your car on the charg -

- er. I just want to see the side, the one that's un - both -

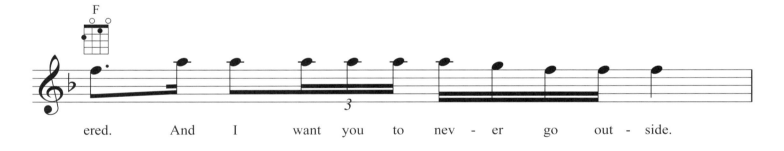

- ered. And I want you to nev - er go out - side.

I prom - ise if they play, my nig - ga's slid - ing.

I'm fuck - ing her and the tour bus still rid - ing.

The Hype

Words and Music by Paul Meany and Tyler Joseph

I don't know which way I'm go - ing, _____ but

I can hear my way a - round. ___ Oh, I can hear my way a - round. _

D.S. al Coda

___ Nice to know _

Coda

hype. Nice to know _

Chorus

___ my _____ kind _____ will be on my side. I don't be - lieve the

hype. And you know __ you're a ter - ri - ble sight, __ but you'll be just

fine. Just don't be - lieve the hype. Nice to know __ hype.

Hey Look Ma, I Made It

Words and Music by Brendon Urie, Dillon Francis, Samuel Hollander,
Michael Angelakos, Jacob Sinclair and Morgan Kibby

First note

Verse
With a groove

1. All my life __ been hus-tling and to - night is my __ ap-prais - al. 'Cause I'm a
2. Friends are hap - py for me, or they're hon-ey-suck - le pho - nies. Then they

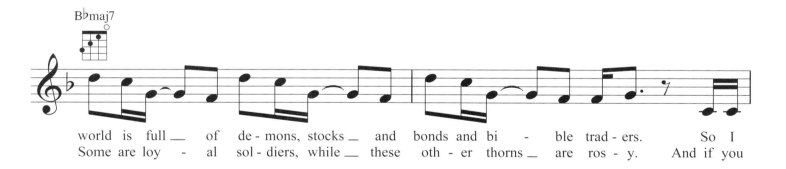

hook - er sell - ing songs and __ my pimp's a rec - ord la - bel. This
cel - e - brate __ my med - als or they wan - na take __ my tro - phies.

world is full __ of de - mons, stocks __ and bonds and bi - ble trad - ers. So I
Some are loy - al sol - diers, while __ these oth - er thorns __ are ros - y. And if you

do the deed, __ get up and leave, __ a climb - er and __ a sa - dist, yeah. __ }
nev - er know __ who you can trust, __ then trust me, you'll __ be lone - ly, oh. __ }

Life in the City

Words and Music by Jeremy Fraites and Wesley Schultz

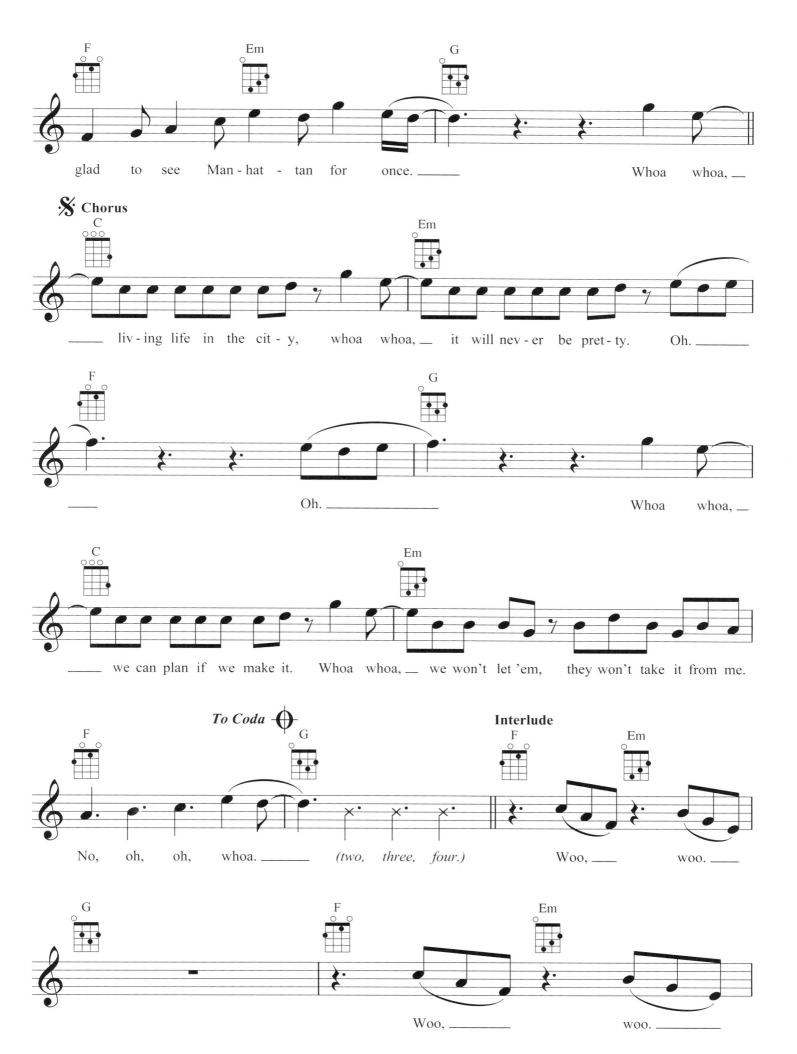

glad   to   see   Man - hat - tan   for   once. _____   Whoa   whoa, _

𝄋 **Chorus**

_____ liv - ing life in the cit - y,   whoa whoa, _ it will nev - er be pret - ty.   Oh. _____

_____ Oh. _____   Whoa   whoa, _

_____ we can plan if we make it.   Whoa whoa, _ we won't let 'em,   they won't take it from me.

To Coda ⊕

No,   oh,   oh,   whoa. _____   *(two, three, four.)*   **Interlude**   Woo, ___   woo. ___

Woo, _____   woo. ___

47

Verse

2. And if you leave, __ don't leave me all a - lone;

__ 'cause I'll be scared, __ I'll be na - ked, I'll get cold.

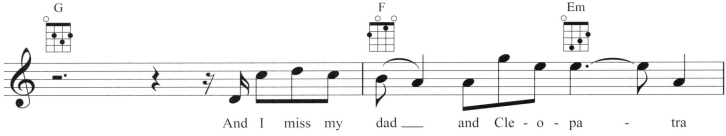

And I miss my dad __ and Cle - o - pa - tra

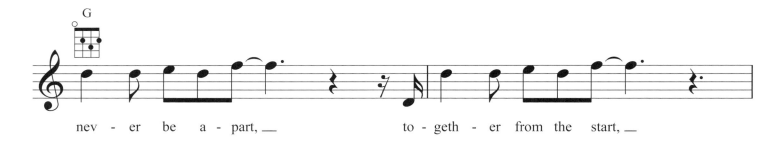

sit - ting on the phone. __ So take me back __ off these __ streets, and we'll

nev - er be a - part, __ to - geth - er from the start, __

D.S. al Coda

nev - er, nev - er fall - ing back a - lone. __ Whoa __ whoa, __

Lose You to Love Me

Words and Music by Selena Gomez, Justin Tranter, Julia Michaels,
Robin Fredriksson and Mattias Larsson

Chorus

We'd al-ways go in-to it blind-ly. I need-ed to lose ___

___ you to find ___ me. This dance, it was kill - ing me soft - ly.

I need-ed to hate ___ you to love ___ me, yeah. To love, love, yeah, to

love, love, yeah, to love, yeah. I need-ed to lose ___

___ you to love ___ me, yeah. To love, love, yeah, to

love, love, yeah, to love, yeah. I need-ed to lose ___

To Coda ⊕

Verse

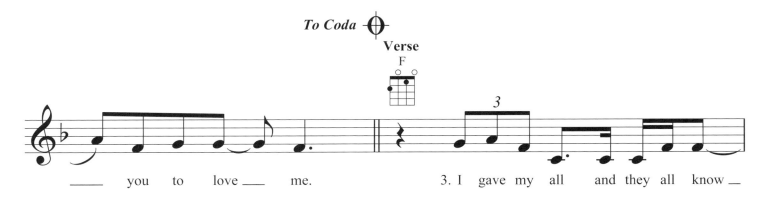

___ you to love ___ me. 3. I gave my all and they all know ___

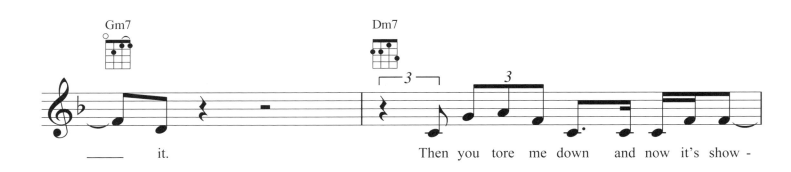

___ it. Then you tore me down and now it's show -

- ing. In two months you re - placed ___ us like it was eas -

D.S. al Coda

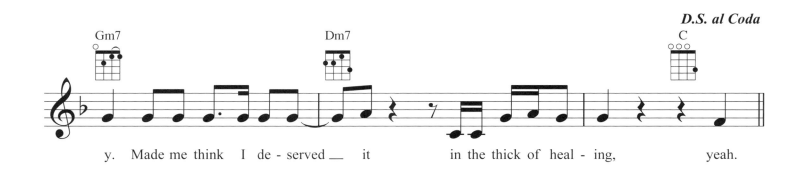

y. Made me think I de - served ___ it in the thick of heal - ing, yeah.

4. You prom - ised the world and I fell for it.

I put you first and you a - dored ____ it. Set fires to my for -

- est, and you let it burn. Sang off - key in my cho -

Outro-Chorus

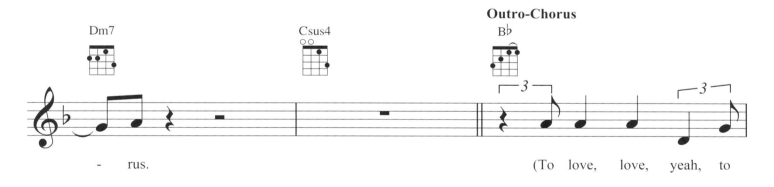

- rus. (To love, love, yeah, to

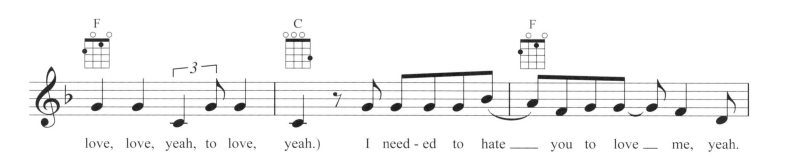

love, love, yeah, to love, yeah.) I need - ed to hate ____ you to love ____ me, yeah.

(To love, love, yeah, to love, love, yeah, to love, yeah.) I need-ed to lose

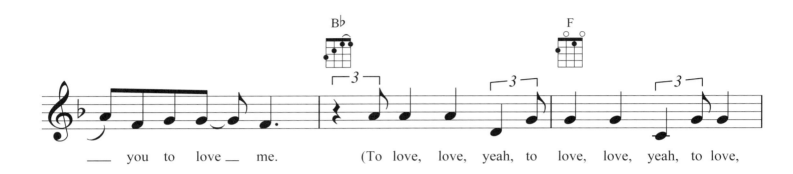

___ you to love ___ me. (To love, love, yeah, to love, love, yeah, to love,

yeah.) And now the chap-ter is closed ___ and done. ___ (To love, love, yeah, to

love, love, yeah, to love, yeah.) And now it's good-bye, it's good-bye for ___ us. ___

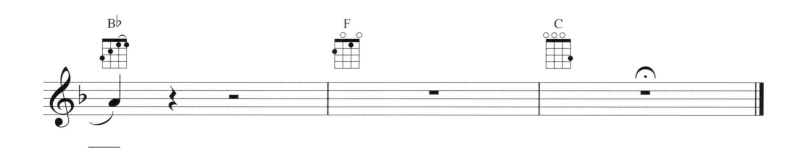

___

Lover

Words and Music by Taylor Swift

First note

Verse
Moderately, in 4

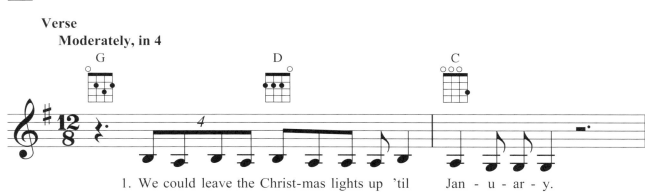

1. We could leave the Christ-mas lights up 'til Jan - u - ar - y.

This is our place; we make the rules. ___ And there's a

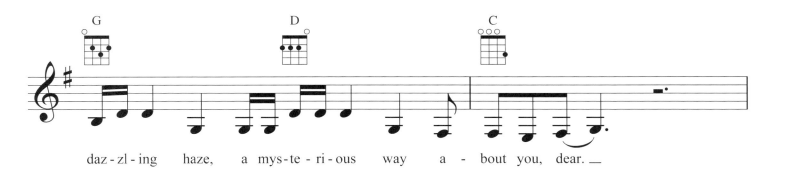

daz - zl - ing haze, a mys - te - ri - ous way a - bout you, dear. ___

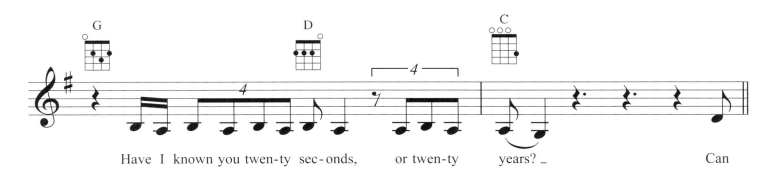

Have I known you twen-ty sec-onds, or twen-ty years? ___ Can

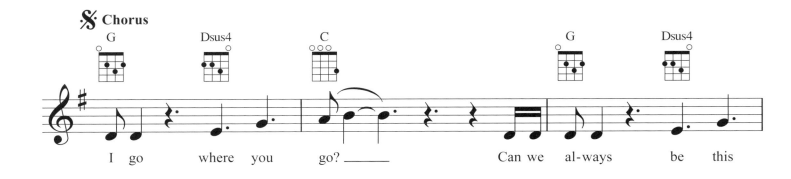

I go where you go? _____ Can we al-ways be this

close? _____ For - ev - er and ev - er, ah, _____ take me out and take me

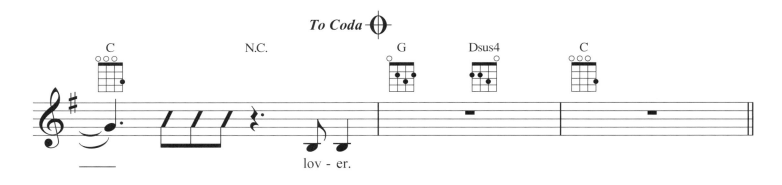

home. _ You're my, _____ my, _____ my, _____ my _____

To Coda

_____ lov - er.

Verse

2. We could let our friends crash in the liv - ing room. _

This is our place; we make the call. __ I'm

high-ly sus-pi-cious that ev-'ry-one who sees you wants _ you. __ I've

D.S. al Coda

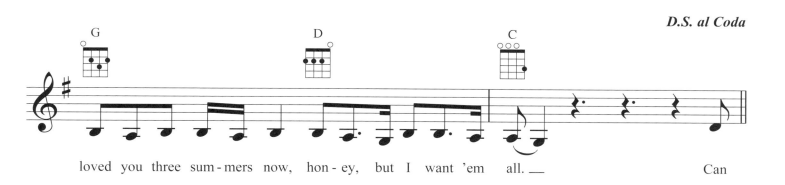

loved you three sum-mers now, hon-ey, but I want 'em all. __ Can

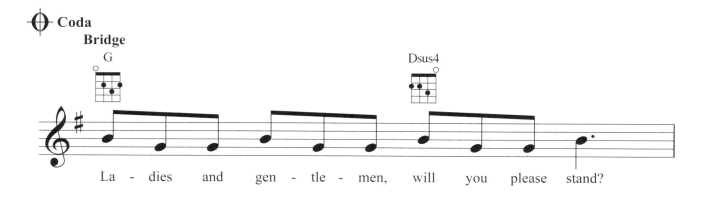

Coda
Bridge

La - dies and gen - tle - men, will you please stand?

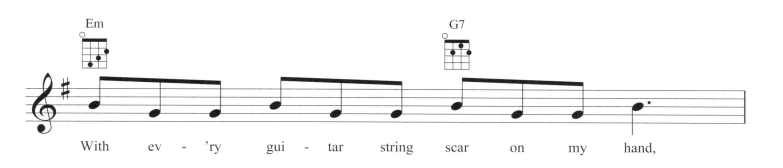

With ev - 'ry gui - tar string scar on my hand,

57

I take this mag - net - ic force of a man to be my lov - er. _____

My heart's been bor - rowed and yours has been blue.

All's well that ends well, to end up with you.

Swear to be o - ver - dra - mat - ic and true ___ to my lov - er. _____ And

you'll save all your dirt - i - est jokes for me. And at ev - 'ry

ta - ble ___ I'll save you a seat, lov - er. _____ Can

Outro-Chorus

I go where you go? _____ Can we

al - ways be this close? _____ For - ev - er and ev - er, ah, __

_____ take me out and take me home. _ You're

my, _____ my, _____ my, _____ my, _____ oh, you're

my, _____ my, _____ my, _____ my, _____ dar - ling, you're

my, _____ my, _____ my, _____ my _____ lov - er.

Memories

Words and Music by Adam Levine, Jonathan Bellion, Jordan Johnson,
Jacob Hindlin, Stefan Johnson, Michael Pollack and Vincent Ford

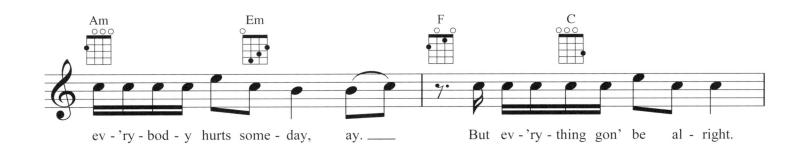

ev - 'ry - bod - y hurts some - day, ay. ____ But ev -'ry - thing gon' be al - right.

Chorus

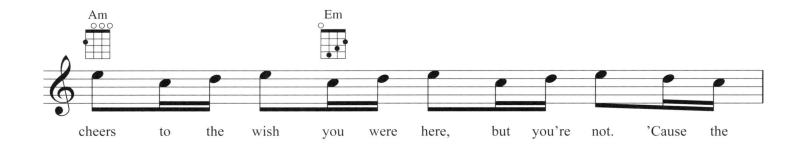

Go and raise a glass and say, ay. Here's to the ones that we got,

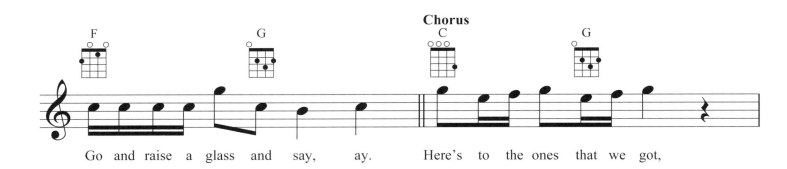

cheers to the wish you were here, but you're not. 'Cause the

drinks bring back all the mem - o - ries of

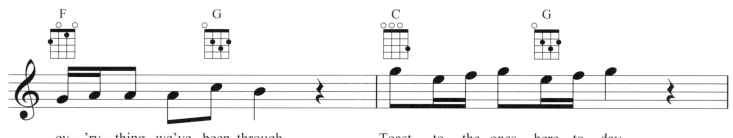

ev -'ry - thing we've been through. Toast to the ones here to - day,

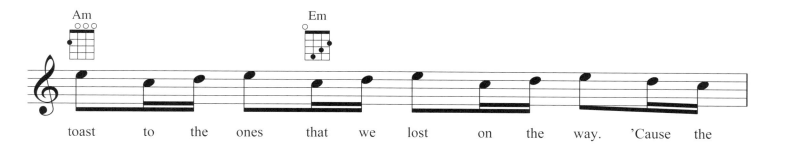

toast to the ones that we lost on the way. 'Cause the

drinks bring back all the mem - o - ries and the

Interlude

mem - o - ries bring back, mem - o - ries bring back you. Do ___ do do do do do.

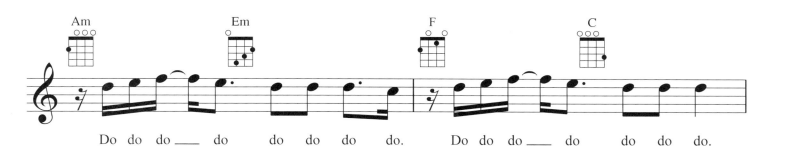

Do do do ___ do do do do do. Do do do ___ do do do do.

1.

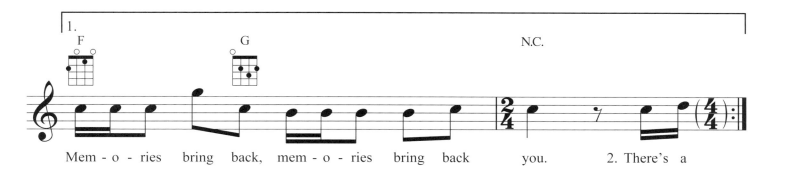

N.C.

Mem - o - ries bring back, mem - o - ries bring back you. 2. There's a

Mem - o - ries bring back, mem - o - ries bring back you. Do — do do do do do.

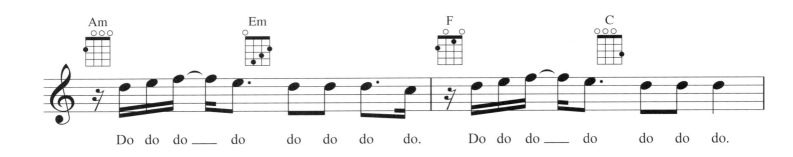

Do do do — do do do do do. Do do do — do do do do.

Outro

Mem - o - ries bring back, mem - o - ries bring back you. Yeah, — yeah, yeah. —

— Yeah, — yeah, yeah, — yeah, doh, — doh.

Mem - o - ries bring back, mem - o - ries bring back you.

Truth Hurts

Words and Music by Lizzo, Eric Frederic, Jesse St. John Geller and Steven Cheung

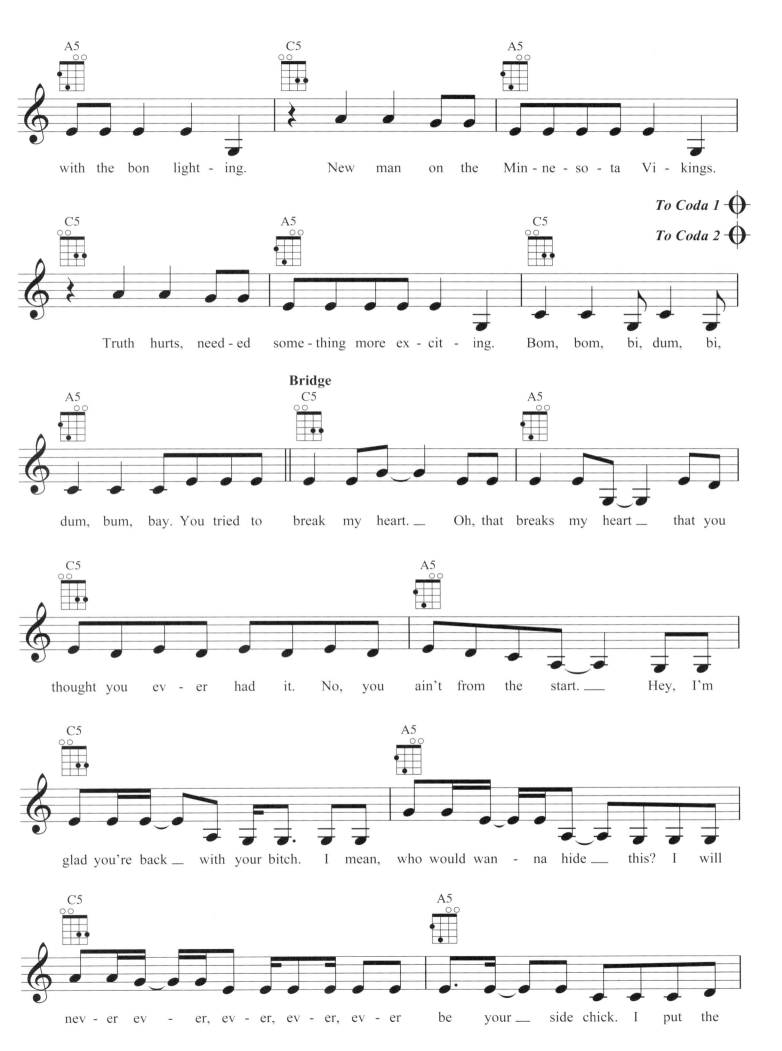

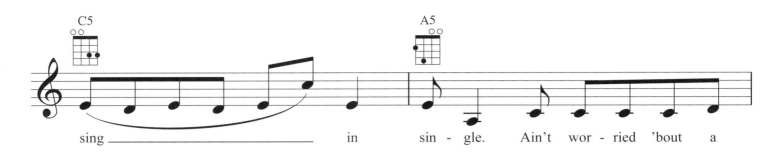

sing _____ in sin - gle. Ain't wor - ried 'bout a

ring _____ on my fin - ger. So you can tell your friend, "Shoot your

D.S. al Coda 1

shot when you see 'em." It's o - kay, he al - read - y in my D - Ms.

Coda 1

Bridge 2

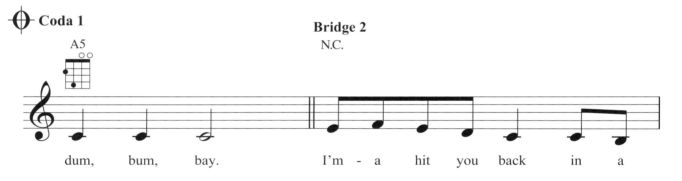

dum, bum, bay. I'm - a hit you back in a

min - ute. I don't play ___ tag, bitch, I been it.

We don't fuck with lies, we don't do good - byes. We just keep it push - in' like

Only Human

Words and Music by Nick Jonas, Joseph Jonas, Shellback and Kevin Jonas

Hurts when I'm leav - in' you, ay. Just

dance in the liv - ing room, love with an at - ti - tude.

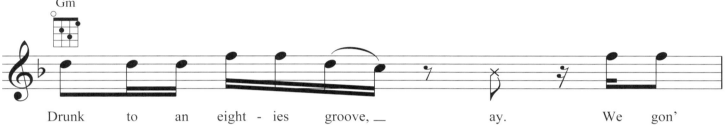

Drunk to an eight - ies groove, __ ay. We gon'

dance in my liv - ing room, slave to the way you move.

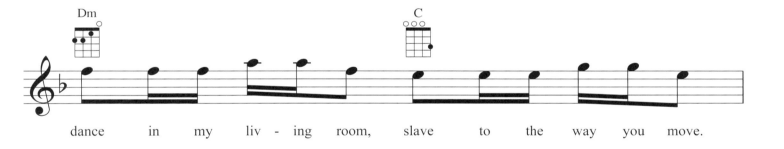

Hurts when I'm leav - in' you, ay. __

Dance in the liv - ing room, love with an at - ti - tude, __ drunk. It's on - ly

Chorus

hu - man, you know that it's real.   So why would you

fight or try to de - ny the way that you feel?   Oh, babe, you can't

fool me. ___   Your bod - y's got oth - er ___ plans ___ so

To Coda

stop pre - tend - ing you're shy,   just come on and dance, ___ dance, ___ dance, ___ dance, ___

Interlude

oh.

Verse

2. Ear - ly morn - in' la - la - light, ___   on -

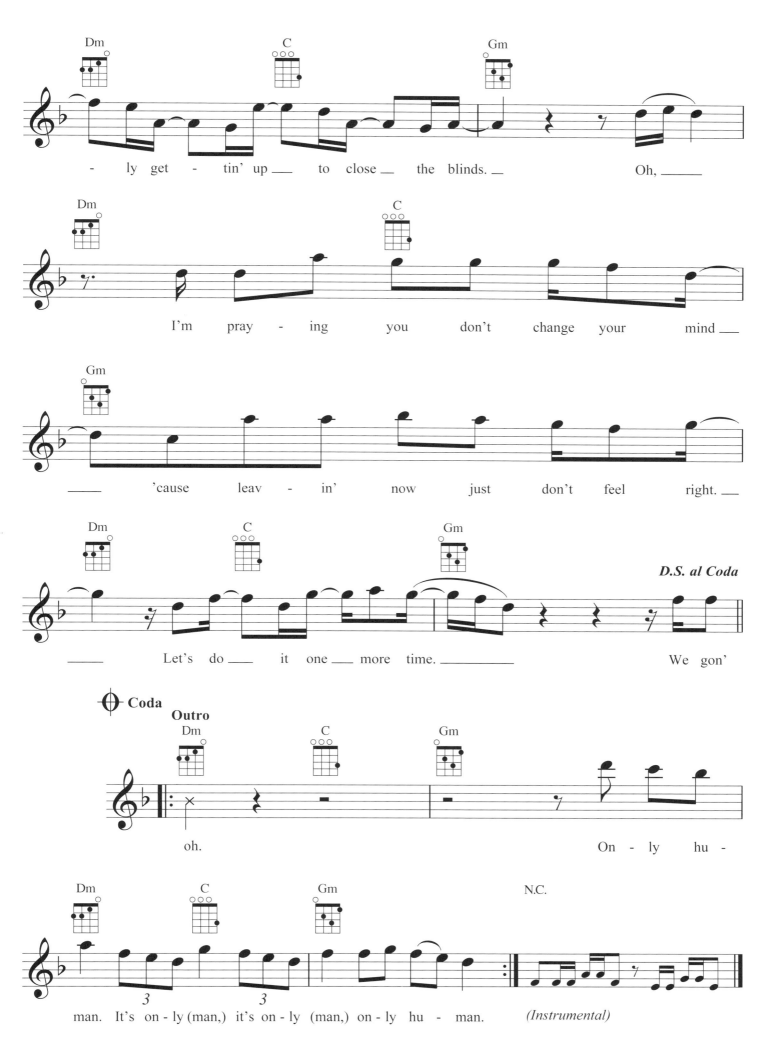

- ly get - tin' up ___ to close ___ the blinds. ___

Oh, ___

I'm pray - ing you don't change your mind ___

___ 'cause leav - in' now just don't feel right. ___

D.S. al Coda

___ Let's do ___ it one ___ more time. ___

We gon'

Coda

Outro

oh.

On - ly hu -

man. It's on - ly (man,) it's on - ly (man,) on - ly hu - man.

(Instrumental)

73

Orphans

Words and Music by Guy Berryman, Jon Buckland, Will Champion, Chris Martin and Moses Martin

Woo, woo, woo, woo, oo, oo, oo.

Cher - u - bim ser - a - phim soon, _____ come

sail - ing us home ___ by the light ___ of the moon. ___

Chorus

I want to know when I can go ___ back and get drunk ___ with my

friends. _____ I want to know when I can go ___

back and feel home ___ a - gain. _____

76

Outro

Woo, woo, woo, woo, oo, oo, oo. _____ I

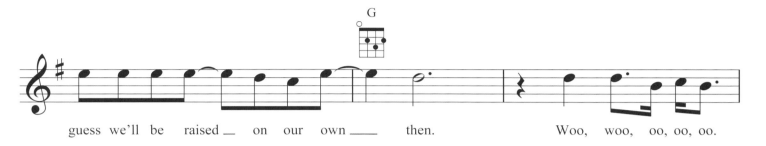

guess we'll be raised ___ on our own ____ then. Woo, woo, oo, oo, oo.

I want to be with you 'til the world _____ ends. ___

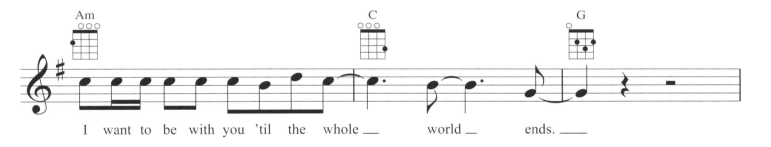

I want to be with you 'til the whole ___ world ___ ends. ____

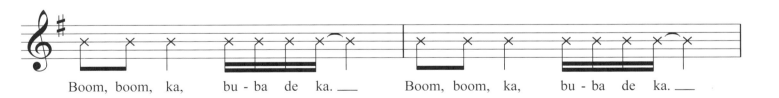

Boom, boom, ka, bu - ba de ka. ___ Boom, boom, ka, bu - ba de ka. ___

N.C.

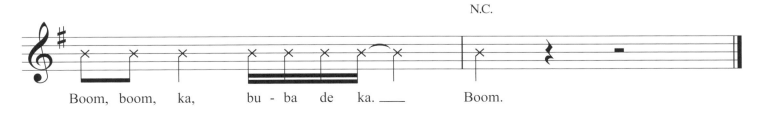

Boom, boom, ka, bu - ba de ka. ___ Boom.

10,000 Hours

Words and Music by Dan Smyers, Jordan Reynolds, Shay Mooney, Justin Bieber, Jason Boyd and Jessie Jo Dillon